Publicado por primera vez por Secret Quay Media Inc. 2015

Copyright M. Gail Daldy 2013 - 2018

Todos los derechos reservados. Ninguna parte de esta publicación puede ser reproducida por ningún medio, bien sea gráfico o electrónico, sin permiso previo y por escrito de la editorial.

Cosas que pasan por Chance | ISBN 978-0-9947957-3-1 | **ESPAÑOL - INGLÉS EDICIÓN**

Series Learn By Chance: Para pedir una copia del libro, envía un email orders@learnbychancebooks.com o llama a 1-604-947-9283

Visítanos en línea en www.learnbychancebooks.com

Director creative: Jason Bamford | Bamford Design | www.bamforddesign.com

Fotografías por Gail Daldy | Traducido por Silvia Xalabarde | Editado por Anne Reid

Un agradecimiento especial a Mark Johnston por todo su trabajo.

Hay un juego de palabras con el título del libro. "Chance" es el nombre del mi hijo, pero también significa "fortuito" o " por casualidad" Las fotos fueron tomadas de esa manera.

Publicado por:
Secret Quay Media Inc.
Box 91194
West Vancouver, British Columbia, Canada
V7V 3N6

www.secretquaymedia.com

Impreso en los Estados Unidos

First published by Secret Quay Media Inc. 2015

Copyright © M. Gail Daldy 2013 - 2018

All rights reserved. No part of this publication may be reproduced in any form or means, graphic, electronic, or mechanical without the prior written permission of the publisher.

Things That Happen By Chance | ISBN 978-0-9947957-3-1 | **SPANISH - ENGLISH EDITION**

Learn By Chance book series: To order a copy of the book email orders@learnbychancebooks.com, or call 1-604-947-9283

Visit us online at www.learnbychancebooks.com

Creative Director: Jason Bamford | Bamford Design | www.bamforddesign.com

Photographs by Gail Daldy | Translation by Silvia Xalabarde | Editing by Anne Reid

A special thank you to Mark Johnston for all of his help.

There is a play on words with the title of the book. "Chance" is the name of my son, but it also means .... the pictures were taken by chance.

Published By:
Secret Quay Media Inc.
Box 91194
West Vancouver, British Columbia, Canada
V7V 3N6

www.secretquaymedia.com

Printed in USA

Lo qué sucedió por Chance

Al mirar fotografías de nuestro hijo Chance de niño, sentí que me transportaban de regreso a su niñez. Como regalo cuando se graduó de la escuela secundaria, pensé que sería divertido reunir una colección de estas fotografías espontáneas en un pequeño libro.

Esta letra ha sido creada utilizando como modelo la letra de algunos de los primeros escritos de Chance en la escuela primaria. Mi esperanza era que pudiera pensar en su niñez y en los momentos especiales, y compartir esas lecciones diarias que aprendió como niño con sus propios hijos. Después de todo, fueron esos momentos los que lo convirtieron en la persona que es hoy.

Espero que disfruten del libro con sus pequeños lectores, y que hablen con una sonrisa de las cosas simples de la vida de las que tanto se aprende.

Un agradecimiento especial
me gustaría agradecer a mis padres el haberme hecho ser consciente de estas pequeñas cosas de la vida.

What Happened By Chance

While looking through some photographs of our son Chance growing up they instantly took me back in time to his early childhood. As my gift to him upon graduating high school I thought it would be fun to put together a collection of these chance snapshots into a little book.

The type face is actually created from some of his earliest hand writing in primary school. My hope was that he would be able to reflect back on his childhood and some of the special moments and share these everyday life lessons that he had learned as a child with his own children. It was these moments after all that made him into the person he has grown up to be.

Hopefully you can enjoy the book with your own little readers and with a smile talk about the simple things in life that teach them so much.

A Special Thanks
I'd like to thank my parents for making me aware of these little things in life.

www.learnbychancebooks.com

Para Chance:

Por regalarme la felicidad más importante para una madre al verte convertirte en ti mismo.

To Chance:

For affording me a mother's ultimate pleasure of watching you become *you.*

Cosas que pasan por Chance
Things That Happen By Chance

Compartiendo lecciones de vida simples con niños en todas partes

Sharing simple life lessons with children everywhere

La vida siempre está llena de pequeñas sorpresas

Life is always filled with little surprises

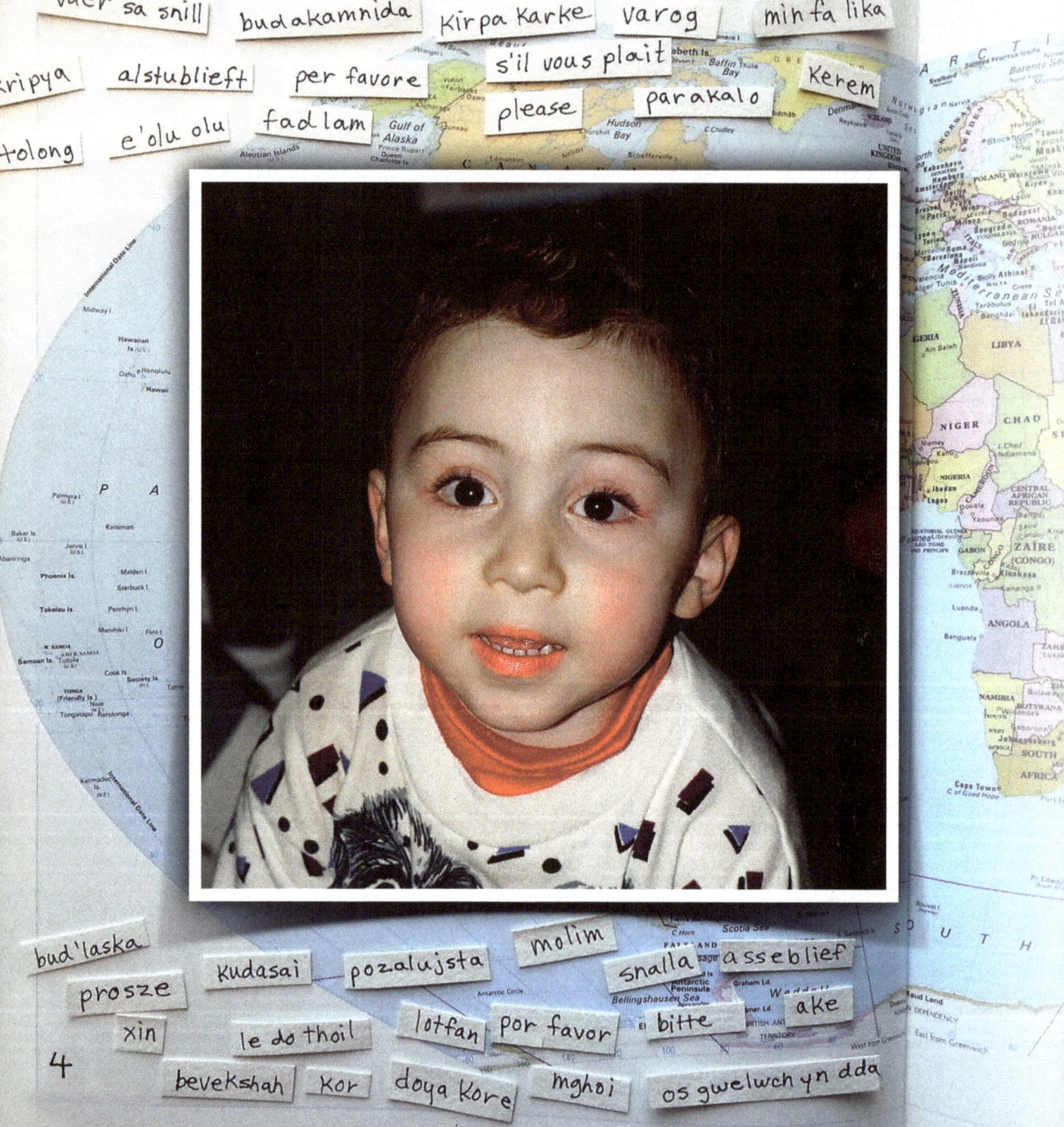

Cuando pidas
algo de alguien
recuerda decir siempre
'por favor'

When you are asking
for something always
remember to say please

Cuando alguien te ayude,
recuerda siempre
sonreír y decir 'gracias'

When someone helps you
always remember to smile
and say thank you

Si mascas chicle,
recuerda 3 cosas :
1. Debe estar dentro de tu boca
2. No lo tragues
3. Nunca lo pongas en tu cabello

If you chew gum
remember 3 things :
1. Keep it in your mouth
2. Don't swallow it
3. Never put it in your hair

Cuando hay algo que hacer
es útil
planear tu ataque

When there is a job
to be done it helps to
plan your attack

Y persistir en él

And stick to it

Hasta el final

Until the very end

No,
creo que no
comí ningún Cheesie

No
I don't think I ate
any cheesies

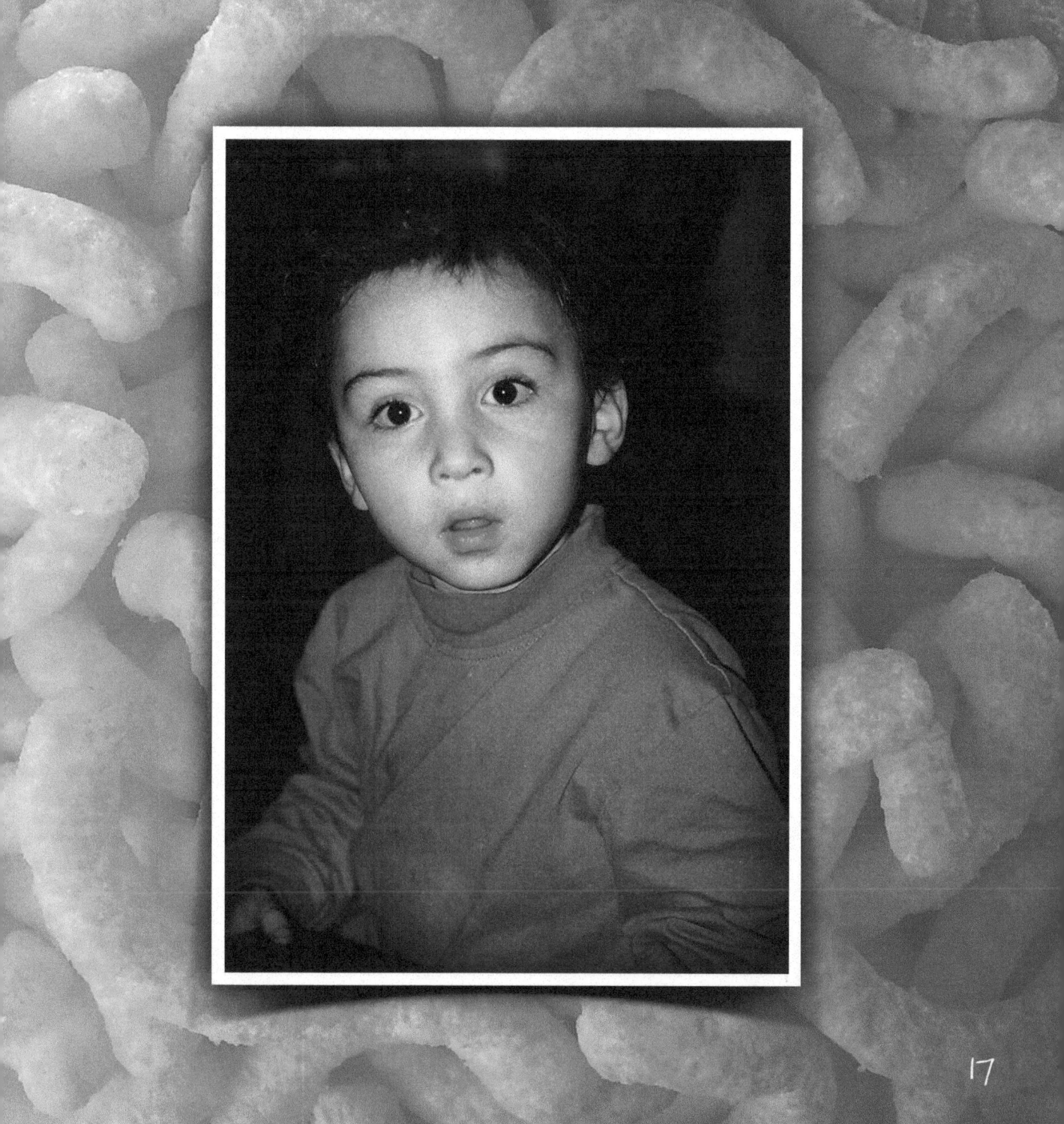

Alimentar
a los pájaros y patos
es muy divertido

Feeding the
birds and ducks
is lots of fun

Pero
no olvides
cerrar la puerta

But don't forget
to close
the gate

Sí,
es posible comer demasiada torta de chocolate

you can eat
too much
chocolate cake

Asegúrate de lavarte los dientes
todos los días
para mantenerlos
limpios y saludables

Be sure to brush your
teeth every day to keep
them clean and healthy

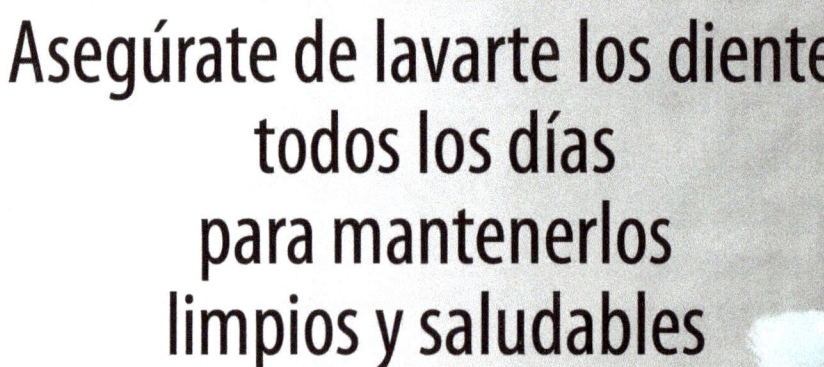

**Los dedos
siempre deben estar
fuera de la nariz**

Always keep your
fingers on the
outside of your nose

Si hay algo de lo que no estés seguro

If there is something you are not sure about

Y alguien o algo
hace que no te sientas bien por dentro,
asegúrate de decírselo a un adulto
inmediatamente

And someone or something
makes you feel not right
inside be sure to tell
a grown up right away

El viento y los truenos de ahí abajo deben hacerse en privado

Wind and thunder
from down under
should be done
in private

Lo siento, fue un accidente

I'm sorry it was an accident

**Es divertido aprender
a hacer galletas**

It's fun learning
how to
bake cookies

**Asegúrate
de mezclar muy bien
todos los ingredientes**

Make sure
you mix all of the
ingredients together
really good

Y recuerda siempre lavarte las manos antes de comenzar

And always remember to wash your hands before you start

Cuando un amigo
necesite a alguien con quien hablar

When a friend
needs someone
to talk to

Intenta siempre escuchar atentamente

Always try
to be a
good listener

Nunca,
nunca jamás
comas nieve amarilla

Never never
ever ever
eat
yellow snow

A veces
la gente cuenta historias
que no son verdad

Sometimes
people tell stories
that are not true

Asegúrate
de que las historias que tú cuentes
sean verdad

Make sure you
tell stories
that are true

**Es divertido
sentir el viento
en el cabello**

It's fun to feel the
wind blow through
your hair

y la arena escurrir
entre los dedos de los pies

and the sand wiggle
between your toes

**Ser amable
hará que tengas
todo tipo de amigos**

Being nice makes
all kinds of
friends

**Cuando cantes,
canta con todo tu corazón**

When you sing,
sing with all
your heart

Cuando tengas la oportunidad, baila

Whenever you get
the chance
just dance

**Y toma siempre tiempo
para detenerte
y oler las flores**

Always take the
time to stop
and smell the flowers

Gracias por leer mi pequeño libro
y por dejarme compartir
algunas de mis lecciones
de vida verdaderas contigo,
Chance

Thank you for reading my
little book and letting me
share some of my real
life lessons with you
by Chance

Sobre la autora

Gail Daldy nació en Chilliwack, British Columbia, en la costa oeste de Canadá, antes de trasladarse a la Isla de Bowen, que está muy cerca de la ciudad de Vancouver. Cuando era joven viajó mucho, experimentando diferentes culturas y modos de vida en numerosos países.

Fue así como se dio cuenta de que los niños de todo el mundo son similares, y pueden aprender unos de otros, y de las cosas simples que les rodean. Ella cree que esta colección de fotografías de Chance captura muchas de esas lecciones de vida diarias, y las muestra de una forma fácil de entender.

About the Author

Gail Daldy was born in Chilliwack, British Columbia on the west coast of Canada before settling on Bowen Island which is just off the Vancouver mainland. As a young woman she travelled extensively experiencing different cultures and everyday living in numerous countries.

From this she realized children are similar the world over and can learn from each other and the simple things that surround them. She believes this collection of chance photographs captures many of these everyday life lessons and illustrates them in an easy to understand way.

Este es el primer libro de la colección Learn by Chance
This is the first book of the Learn by Chance series.

"Kids will really relate to the photos in this book, and be both inspired and amused." - Temple Grandin, Author, *Thinking in Pictures*

"These masterful photographs with entertaining and clever text makes "Things That Happen By Chance" a perfect book to impart useful knowledge to a young child and start wonderful conversations." - Tom Best, Executive Director, *First Book Canada*

"A delightful addition to our Reach Out and Read program!"
- Dr. Laurie Green, *Reach Out and Read Canada*

Things That Happen By Chance

To say "A picture is worth 1000 words" seems so cliché while at the same time appropriate in pointing out the obvious in this little book of Chance.

As seen through the eyes of one little boy a growing visual interactive experience of a child learning simple life lessons that can be shared with children all over the world.

Seeing and reading about his adventures as they happen creates a great conversation opener for parents giving them an opportunity to talk about similar enjoyable moments and lessons learned with their own children.

GAIL DALDY

Taking a closer look at the little things in life

learnbychancebooks.com

SPANISH
ENGLISH
EDITION

$18.95 USD | for ages 2 & up
ISBN 978-0-9947957-3-1
COPYRIGHT 2013 - 2017 © SECRET QUAY MEDIA INC. | ALL RIGHTS RESERVED | PRINTED IN USA

www.ingramcontent.com/pod-product-compliance
Lightning Source LLC
Chambersburg PA
CBHW061930290426
44113CB00024B/2866